Crop Circle Secrets

Crop Circle Secrets

poems by

Thomas Hastings

The Muse Rules
Indianapolis

Acknowledgments

Some of these poems appeared in prior chap-books by Thomas Hastings:

1974   *Amulets*, Liberal Arts Press, Baltimore
1977   *When I Danced*, Free University Press, Indianapolis
1979   *Cynosure*, Raintree Press, Bloomington
1980   *Political Love Poems*, Writers Center Press, Indianapolis
1981   *Thin Times*, Fly-by-Night Press, Bloomington
1983   *Ansiru Comments*, Ink Press, Bloomington
1985   *Vertical Sleep, Horizontal Lies*, Fly-by-Night Press, Bloomington
1988   *Unfinished Things*, Matchbooks #2, Unionville
1990   *Martial Law* (with Marty Belcher), Matchbooks #15, Unionville
2000   CoupCoupDaddy Compact Disc

Thomas Hastings' work has also appeared in the *Indianapolis Broadsheet, Inprint, IndiAnnual, The Windless Orchard, Aloe, Banyon Anthology #2,* and the *Linen Weave Anthology.*

Cover Design by Ursina Hastings-Heinz

All Rights Reserved.

Copyright © 2004 by Thomas Hastings

The Muse Rules: a literary press
715 Northview Avenue
Indianapolis, IN 46220

ISBN 0-9713615-5-X

CONTENTS

Magician	3
Obolos	4
Leaving the Next Day	7
Zocolo	8
Alacrity	9
The Mood of Good Food	10
Under the Full New Year Moon	12
Stitch and Shine	13
Mas o Menos	14
All Around Square	16
The Whole Goddamn Story	18
Chronoclutch	22
Later, in France	25
In Basel	26
Zurich Bahnhof	28
Psephology	29
All As Is	30
Clarification	31
Isso and Ellen	33
They Live Above	34
All the Bills	35
Ellen Wants	36
Isso Worries	37
Isso Finds a Note	38
Telecommunications	39
Isnot	40
Anecdotal Requests	41

Isnot Desires	42
That Old Sleep Hag	43
Isso Dreams	44
Dear Ellen	45
Isso's Journals End	46
Sober	47
Solara Velossa	48
Transfinity	49
Lumine	51
Genome	52

Older Work

The Landing	54
Obsidian	56
L	58
Opus	59
Transforming the Gold	60
The Mating	61
Dusk	62
Zurich	63
When I Danced	64
Corn Mother	65
Simple as That	66
What It Is	67
Hidden Indian	68
Spooks	69
Hunger	71
Good Friday	72
Wild Geese Pass	73

for ursina and natasha

Magician

here's what happens next

after the ufos are exposed
the weird people live in peace
on the mountain top

the clowns of zurich go on tour
overnight wiry hair
grows on my left shoulder

in my fever you're there
we stroll the streets with athens
like loose change in our pockets

horned ones caught
in the zigzag lightning

nacreous smudge
of apollo's thumb
on aurora's thigh

we're here in their
extrasensory
deprivation tank

cards in hand
waiting to deal

Obolos

confidence man
cool coin slide

how to get the
freshly minted
carefully borrowed

coin from one
place to another

shall it go from
breast pocket to
bottom of shoe

or appear in
a nest of
lacquered chinese boxes

manifest inside
a ball of mother's yarn

go up in a flash
with alchemical charm

squeeze between
the pasteboard layers
of a king

has the card
been forced or
randomly selected

hell you can sell
a magician a pencil
that doesn't write

here it is
now it's gone

it's still here
no it's not

Leaving the Next Day

in my dream on the way
to the airport at the tollbooth
on 110 near leon
I was shot by soldiers
with machine guns
unafraid
in my dream it was night
and leaving the next day
sylvano the taxi driver
didn't know the names
of the scraggly trees
bursting cotton phosphorus

Zocolo
(for sweetheart the clown)

in this thresh-held square
you comfort the old man
selling lemonade from his cart
visited twice by spirits
on the day of the dead

the old flower woman
plucks change from my palm
what will you do
with these marigolds

you lie down
with the napping dog
tickle its nose
cameras click and whir

you peek under the veil
of the passing funeral procession
go for lunch with friends

later, I get my first shoeshine
at six o'clock sharp
the birds go amuck

Alacrity

at the flamenco restaurant
the grumpy gourmet returns
the half-frozen artichoke

assesses it at the windchill factor
of elizabeth dole's liver

it gets nuked and returned
sunblocked in the ruins

cousin wolf laments an omnipresence
of pushup bras after spending

his christmas bobbing on a beach
of bronzed nipples pointing true north

he requests the band to play adelita
pancho villa's favorite marching song

waiters serve with more alacrity
in san miguel you tip accordingly

how slow your taxi goes
weight gets measured again

delivers us to the house of looms
mother of rugs
her barefoot daughters

The Mood of Good Food

pork rinds big
as robert bly's vest
tasty with salsa

rumor of barbecue cabrito
roadside breakfast
early before ten

sautéed cactus, scallop cerviche
fruitjuice with gas
bitter coffee from chiapis

a shameless go at veal
with apples and noodles
surrounded by well-meaninged poets

steaming corn on the cob
lime rubbed, mayo slathered

cheese rolled, chili jolted
offered to salty aztec noon

but the steak at julien's
with or without the béarnaise

filet the size of my two fists
seared on childhood's savory grill

blesses the sacred cowherd's maidens
tends volcano, stirs the stirrer

endows the settling afternoon
one last bite

Under the Full New Year's Moon

fireworks tonight
tumbleweeds polish speed bumps

a fly egg laid in an officer's horse's ear
cracks open the church like a ripe piñata
at a bad news laundromat

missing clerical collars
nun's dirty habits flutter to the street

surgical needles embroider
your song on the grape's eyelid

and you don't want to leave
no you can't bear to leave

only at the ocean do you find
that small wooden guitar
you so want to play

Stitch and Shine

pesky pluto shifting orbits
vows to keep persephone

demeter trades inside stock market tips
damage control for solar storm gossip

the waking world tends to its own

you must abandon
your father's sheepskin coat

wear his passion's ruby ring

Mas O Menos

mayan paradise, poolside bar
strom thurmond swears in william rhenquist

rome, juno moneta is turning tricks
in the cloakroom again

mexico city, billy graham transforms
coral snakes into genuflecting oil derries

time magazine, international edition
with sobriety and fluidity
the homoculus poses in the alembic races

quiera la quenta, por favor
quiero el quento, quiero el quento

All Around Square

like a dog's bad dream
ted turner on all fours
lapping blood from a fallen
satellite dish

new peek technique
weight of sunlight
on a cornfield
its magnetic intent

svaha—sanscrit interlude
between lightning and thunder
greetings mathematical anomaly

intellectual property protected
by computer generated image
counterintuitive probabilities
hypertext transfer protocol

the owners are betting
their turquoise teeth
bubbles and strings
are popping and twanging

electric force does not fall off
with the distance squared
whose hand rests
in the jaguar's mouth

cnn's candy crowley
does cyberspace
for the first time
recites the starr report
live off worldwide web

in the old days we'd kill the king
if he didn't ask for a blowjob
every now and then

iridium-husked martian worms
crashland the polar cap

soldiers disguised as
telephone repairpersons
explode in the olive grove

gourds explore
the city dumps

luna moths feed
on the dragon's eyes

The Whole Goddamn Story

Prologue:

we picked up something
they called my brother in clovis
to come and pick it up

of course at one point
we turned it into a carrier pigeon
attacked by a hawk

my wife nursed it back to health
we let it go
and that was that

but the symbols leaked
along with the curious properties
the debris possessed

you know, ezekiel saw the wheel
way up in the middle of the air
turned by god...turned by faith?

you try walking into the wind
with your arms full of blazing tumble-
weeds
then, when we realized
the yuccas were transmitters, well...

--"carl bad," roswell, 1982

bando sigma snowbird pounce
1949's project grudge
gave bigfoot the brushoff
hired a shrink for the missing link

1952's majestic-12, magic,
where there's foo, there's fire
sister capistrano says its so—
twisted her wing in the deus exmachina

foxtrot kilothree zero blue
orthon and the mothership
fared well in '52, allen dulles
warned off lawsuits against the contactee

after the medicine men told nasa
not to bring the moon rocks home—
lordy, how they've grown

'75's travails of travis in navajoland
snowflake, arizona chupacabra
munching up his plasma vortext
another electronically disturbed day

pitchblende, bell raspings,
swamp gas and soot
hierograms from the glory hand

dowse your rod and grid
with sorcerer's grease
loop the leylines, ride the spoors
to the dogstar's dawn

on the way to rishekish
sadhus, gurus, babas,
bagwans, anandas

pay maharishi mahish
ten thousand u.s. dollars
join the yogi mafia
learn to fly

or be like lord buckley—
bungie off the bicameral bridge
sailin' and wailin' seratonin

follow kundalini down
back to his orphic egg
the farthest outer other ever anywhere

snap back at the ranch
nords and morlocks
blondes and greys
identified alien craft

incoming incunabulum
1899's coney island's dreamland
circus sideshow and universal
congress of freaks

the quotidian wonders of colonel joy
his contact muscle reading
his telepathic punch swazzle

ninety miles outside of lucky las vegas
the whole skunkaroo, the ranch . . .
human containers and leakers groomed

auger by the river of zero point energy
microwave relay, cellular link
mission critical system
codeboot: timeloss, disassociation

coronal discharge fractals
dance behind the satellite's footprints
airbrushed silent blue

Chronoclutch

it all began with the banana man
cornucopiating on captain kangaroo
profondes and pochettes softly bulging
black and white produced his green world

univac arranged romance
folks played cyanide roulette
on the people are funny show

long before a teenaged billy graham
got god on the eighteenth hole,
before the sphinx and carnac's temple
began to wither into lime

an idle crowd of parvenus
gathered to watch the sale
of retorts, crucibles, elixirs

pharoah's eggs and sooner pills
a shovel of ether perched on coals
and the boy levitates

we knew how to prepare
the flesh-colored paint
so it would not glow

we hired carpenters
to build new spirit cabinets
rather than tote them
from town to town

we'd procure the local chief's friendship
to embolden our territorial patois and po-
litesse
protect our handbill's modest claims

ours was a clean spookshow
just off by a century or two
the world's most expensive dream

we still seek the old stone
purveyors of feathers and camel drop-
pings
we are dusting the oasis for fingerprints

Later, in France

traffic slowed on our way
to the strasbourg cathedral

men in orange suits were moving
the bridge of three roses

light northerly rain
from the black forest
stippled the rhine

an old woman on bicycle
tapped on the window
gave me advice in swiss

embrace jesus
or end up like her

her license plate read *esprit*

later, in france,
ululation

In Basel

in the new moon's shallop
from bomb craters gather
gall and wormwood

timothy and witchgrass
polyphemus, cicropia
roma, sinta, zeiguner

tarot trackers, bear trainers
caldron roilers, hot car traders

the perilous crossings of roses
sunflowers by a hydro dam

when the seven become one
the work is finished

caretakers place the son's bones
in a golden jar with the father's

a terrible whitening
a bleaching out of good

brilliantly colored microscopic life
leaves the coral reefs

dolphins are biting tourists
pulling them under
eating their young

french halogenic light
dazes cleopatra's boudoir
eurodollars leak like mir

rogue planets, orphan planets
progeny of tumultuous birthings
roam sans sun

dense atmospheres protecting
molecular hydrogen's longing
for lumen naturae

on a street corner in basel
paracelsus whispers
from the polyglotal jaws
of the dragon, *drink*

bubba at pine ridge
hilary jerusalem
jesse bearing glad rags
from macedonia

jimmy carter onto jacarta
assumptio maria
mistress of creation
assumptio maria
mistress of creation

Zurich Bahnhof

peer up at the equilibrist
tiny headed winged swollen body

of temperance ambidextrously
pouring her wine into wine

po mista bubba
got da deep downs now

cassandra catapults
her poison spacepill elsewhere

covert plutonium diffuses soil
around gaseous paducah

north korean nano-neutrons sight
alaskan strip malls

arms dealers give themselves
another great hand—yours

how to get out of the enchanted castle
what number to enter the empath chan-
nel

look, I have a magic cow
I'll trade her for your lousy beans
93 million terrorist miles from home

Psephology

liddy's bully pulpit
junior's papal bull
do he do voodoo too

just imagine, zobop
bizango, macandahl
meet in obidiah

past demonic possession
of presidential aspirants
is not a pretty thing

just too many dry wells
and even call me alpha al
claims he's a child of the kingdom

last year a meteorite's primordial
water locked inside halite crystal
whistled and whomped into texas
flinging creation's salt
all over the swan maiden's tail

the swamps is burnin'
but the troops is comin' home

we'll build more prisons
for free radicals
rehabilitate eternity

All As Is

now half the babies
in parts of africa have aids

and women are just learning
they are not owned

by their fathers or husbands
or sons

one third of the world is teenaged now

and sound waves are visible
on jets' wings just before they hit mach

twelve million gypsies inhibit europe

the man who made voices
come from his hands has died
at the age of one hundred and three

and more will be known
about that strange light
no one knows
comes or goes

Clarification

you can't cheat the old ones
you must give
a little this, a little that
all away

the owners call this
capital gain and
give the bone people
shiny swords and
hard dancing horses

afterwards, the caretakers
shoulder the spent props
the scenery, carry them
all away

the chorus asks
how can
zero come first
much less
spirit or soul

isso and ellen
set up household
in my head

swooshing brooms
scatter the clinging
pronouns

tonight the hermit's lamp
will direct restless
warriors

isso's journal entry
will reflect the light
back

they live above a garage
and know nothing about cars

isso makes a list
of all the animals and people

and places cars
are supposed to be

he uses colored inks
for the abstract ones

ellen draws tiny horses
on her toenails

all the bills are paid
by the mechanic downstairs

he works out with gyroscopes
and has a faded tattoo of a lemniscate

or is it a pair of handcuffs

ellen wants to do stand up
it's driving isso crazy

he doesn't understand timing
power confuses him

he wants the pope to buy
hong kong for the dalai lama

he thinks stillborn watches
are prayer wheels

isso worries about the solar wind
stopping last may

he wonders if there is a toggle switch
he should know about

last time the northern lights
showed up this far south

was 1959 the year american scientists
patented the computer chip

isso remembers giving away his drums
and no more dance lessons

isso finds a note tucked
into his journal

it's from the mechanic
who's fixed the roof:

"couldn't do anything
with the missing vent

but tightened
your gutter spikes

if ellen wants to shoot
some glue into the cracks

on the porch
it will only help"

a telecommunications sales agent
offers isso a magnetiscope

a home study course
in neurolinguistic deception

sleight-of-hand's advantage
with two second delay

psychological and manipulative
mastery guaranteed

isso pluralizes the lifetime
warranty and signs

and signs
and signs

isso's brother isnot dwells
in the witches' house

never leaves without
his poison breadcrumbs

to feed his neuroses
find his way back

isnot knows not
how old he is

he knows the months
are somehow marked

perhaps the mechanic
can fashion
special glasses

he's begun to email
furtive anecdotal requests
seeking stories of old mentors

the mustachioed senator
the reverend mindreader

his old buddies
jesse james and ulysses grant

isnot demands to know
how magnetic fields work

what hovers above
the magician's head and strength

where have the men
on four horses gone

isnot desires new patter notions
revisions of gemini kings
the professor's twisting the aces

isnot wonders how many pins
will dance on an angel's head

he wants to strike a happy medium
hard

that old sleep hag kanashihari
is after isnot

to escape he must evade
the temporal lobes

crawl down the corpus collosum
and hotwire the hypothalamus

with his dangerous cheerfulness
he leaps astride the joker's epaulettes

bicycles into polymer modulators
slows into copper iron tin lead

and somersaulting upside down
an alphabet spills from his forehead

while isso dreams of the halcyon
the last of the appalachian beat poets

murmurs when whales hear sonar
they think it's little voices

ellen centerdeals solitaire
each card one thread thick
she misses her winged orb

she misses topping
the juggler's next toss

serpentine hair ribbons
torn and restored

she knows sacrifice
means making sacred

hushing the struggle
of a fixed mean sun's logic

dear ellen,

isso's thrown his back out
messing with my gyros

he's ok resting upstairs
practicing shadowgraphy
with hexaflexagrams

yesterday I discovered
a radioactive black diamond
in a belgian import's carburetor

don't fret—lunch won't tick
isnot's lead shields us

last night little egypt ferried me
up the salamander river in her
vessel of willow and mastadon bone

she returned with this letter
and to get silver coins

isso will fill in the details
see you later

> the mechanic
> luna park
> 6/22/08

isso's journals end
the amanuensis is not

the origin of transmission
isnot is not isnot

he's been to mars
and brought back mousewoman

she fell through the roof
of his test one module gazebo

she has an empty bag
inside her womb

to undo the names
of the tiniest things

the knights' horses have been found
in japan, france and italy

the silence of chung ling soo
arrives from the miracle factory

sober for seven years
isso declines the beers
café phlumlis, lime schnapps
intriguing kirsch-laced pastries
he bids chablis-dunked bread cubes
a fondue adieu

he provides inner sanctuary
for his drunken ones
and monitors their
squelps and screeps
on his wound-to-wound endoplasm scale

isnot warns isso
if he's going to carouse
the calendars, he better not
expect his horoscope
to stay put

ellen and isso have a daughter
her name is solara velossa she says
she's eight years old

imagine, isso a soccer dad
stumbling over buckyballs in nanotubes
floating away and popping with birthday
bubbles

solara excels at cat's cradle and negotia-
tion
her motto is: plans change fast

solara asks isso
what comes after infinity

he asks around
transfinity he tells her

where's heaven then
she wants to know

before infinity he replies
fair enough

Lumine

dr. hau slows light
stops it cold

in gas, a second
beam revives the first

and things can be
two places at once

electromagnetically
induced transparency

                    isso liwok
                    1/01/01

Genome

justice, blindsided by the chariot
drops her sword on temperance

the hurtling blade cleaves
the elixer's parabola

plummets and disrupts
its whirling axis

glaciers calve and boom
fossil gears begin to click

delicate play of rod and cone
rasp of atropos opening her sissors

just enough time to breach
the glistening universe

busy clothos tallies
our genetic score:

devil 24, magician 23, moon 23,
fool 19, lovers 18, death 17

ellen elpy
1/01/08

Older Work

The Landing

passing on
to the next caldera
flying a kite
from the volcano's mouth
I find the beast
here in this calefactory
pulling the taut string
alternating the protean masks
of demon and seraphim
marmorial voices inculcate
nihil obstat, nihil obstat
dew crowns the thorn
ram's blood flows from the trees
vision opens the eyes
of the herm
sight beside itself
the vessel is lowered
into the fire
the flame burns
green and gold
bones grow out
leave the body
circuit, rune merge
the shimmering feathers
of peacocks smoke
like the pattern
surrounding all things

chameleons graze, change
their skins in unison
dragonflies skim
the calm waters
with only the tips
of their singing bodies
now I am inside the bullroarer
no longer the automatic nerve
of sacrifice wincing
in the dark raw bowl
the scream frozen
to the bell thaws
mistletoe laurels oak
there is a certain species
of bees, I am told,
that climbs to a great height
each beltane, then mates
in freefall ricocheting
through the atmosphere

Obsidian

when you are reflected
in this semi-precious gem
everything is seen
through a heat wave
your face is moss
tarnishing a tree
beneath this tree
a young woman is standing
she weeps your name
and the landscape
ceases breathing
lying near her swaying feet
you see the body of a bull
the rib the young woman
draws from its side
drones like an oud in her hands
it is the shape
of a snowflake's hinge
through which you may step
onto the darker side
she offers it you
but you cannot grasp it
the room in which you sit
exits so quietly reflected
in this semi-precious gem
a clock in a temple growing faint
with its own ticking
night sings into the wound

it is this voice the blood follows
a plant springs from a stone
a glacier quickens pace
geodes blossom in its path

L

a slight skirmish
amid shrewd constellations
cigarette holder held aloft
she slipped on the orange
and fell off the bed
coughing and laughing
don't smoke it anymore sweet
fires will still crackle in your laurel
the ashtrays are passed you
the histories the poses
you remember all your bodies
do you have any lipstick she asks me
hands busy brushing glitter
from the sheets the restless evening

Opus

when earth finally flexes its poles
i do not believe any bees will fall
nor will any skin be sloughed
though things will crawl about
a bit differently
i celebrate the diamond's hatching
it will make less sound
than the resurrection of coal

Transforming the Gold

you have a high regard
for the sleeping mind
oh dreamer

transforming the gold
back into lead
for smuggling

The Mating

my wife with red hair
who lives in africa
catches fish with her teeth
then lies with the river
she opens her legs
my wife with red hair
and my grandmother's house burns

Dusk

at dusk there is weeping
men beating starfish
with the bones of old women
stranded on beaches of salt
shores froth at their mouths
young women look on
brush one another's hair
turtles carry light back into the sea
stones rise to the surface

Zurich

there are no more beasts
in the forests of switzerland
they snuck into the pastures
ate the cows and sheep
and were killed long ago
by men in grief
wounding their assassins
now only the franc slays
old men sit
surrounded by alps
in the vaults of gold
giggling and rubbing their hands
old women snore
leaves scrape the sidewalk

When I Danced

i leapt out of my shoes
i leapt out of my pants
i leapt out of my belly
the radio was square
i leapt out of the room
i forgot my shirt
i left it tied
around your waist

Corn Mother

dark moth pale wall
hand holds lamp barn glows
rafters sheaves indian corn
roof rain horse she rides
corn husk into the forehead
she rides the rain she rides the sun
and sets in the one who dwells there

Simple As That

taking the single breath
leaves fall cupped to earth
seasons change inside the body
the bell inside the body rings
the body rings simple as that
in the garden the wishing well
spits out its coins

What It Is

it is
an electric alarm clock
not the sun
moon stars
waking you

it is
a garbage disposal
not what
earth can
do well
by herself

it is
an air conditioner
not a crazy wind
blowing through
a brick wall

Hidden Indian

there's this cherokee
who follows me
telephones
when I'm in the shower
tells me
of other baptisms
no darkness
to wash away
no darkness
only night

building a fire
tells me
my masculine rage
when I put on
my suit each morning
with its pockets
of flames

Spooks

she thinks this
can't be happening
will the tornado's eye
seek her out
years from now
in some dim
forsaken trailer court
seize a part
of her she thought
finally protected

perhaps it is
her dreamself playing tricks
taped light switches
don't stay down
dresser drawers pout
from her bedroom
dishes rattle
at church elders
the scent of lilacs
fills the air

candles swoon
coffee cups crash
her sister's prom picture
flies off the wall

a telephone receiver
floats across the
teenager's lap
stretches taut
of its own accord
in her living room
of many phones

Hunger

hummingbird
feeding from
bamboo
wood chime

Good Friday

spring rain
the canoe
fills with water
in the backyard

Wild Geese Pass

one splitting
logs pauses
prying the axe
from the wood's grip

About the Author

Hoosier born and braised, Thomas Hastings was poetry editor of the *Indianapolis Broadsheet* and the Writers' Center of Indianapolis *In-Print* magazine. He is known for his lively performances and lectures. For the past twenty-six years, he has taught language arts, gender psychology and theatrical magic at Harmony School in Bloomington, Indiana. He may also be Googled through "mythogenics" or the film "Voyage to Arcturus".